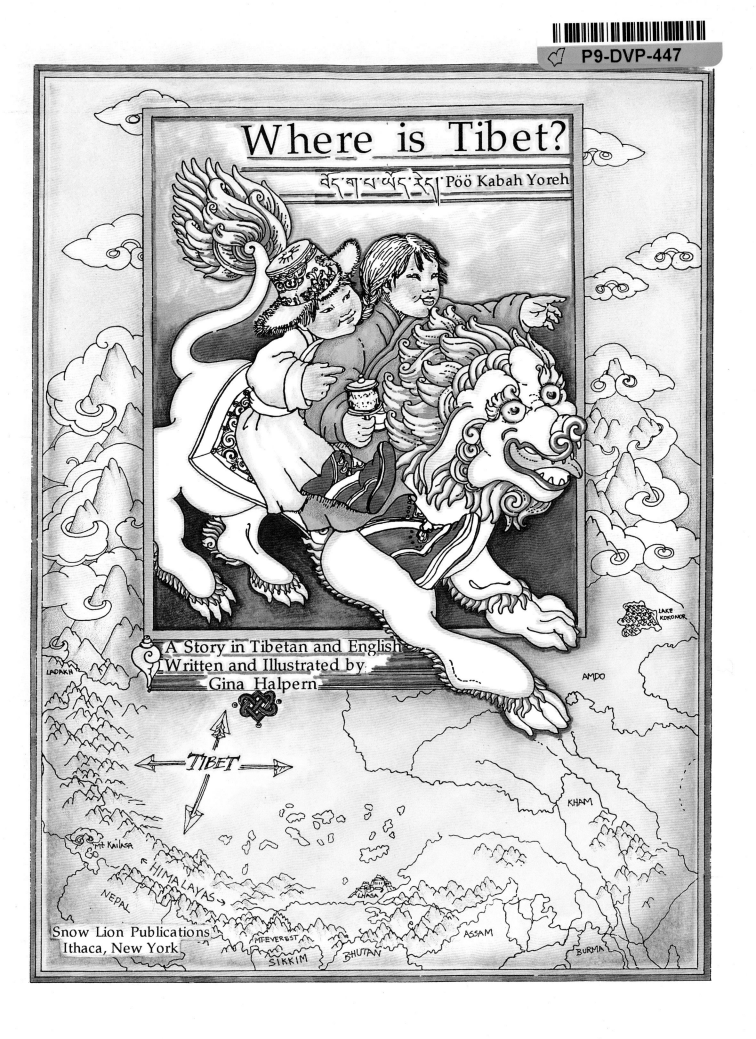

Where is Tibet?

བོད་ག་བ་ཡོད་རེད། Pöö Kabah Yoreh

A Story in Tibetan and English
Written and Illustrated by
Gina Halpern

LADAKH

TIBET

mt KAILASA

HIMALAYAS

NEPAL

LHASA

MT. EVEREST

SIKKIM

BHUTAN

ASSAM

BURMA

KHAM

AMDO

LAKE KOKONOR

Snow Lion Publications
Ithaca, New York

Snow Lion Publications
P.O. Box 6483
Ithaca, NY 14850
USA

Printed in Singapore
ISBN 0-937938-94-7 {cloth}
ISBN 0-937938-93-9 {paper}

Library of Congress Cataloging-in-Publication Data

Halpern, Gina, 1951-
Where is Tibet? = Bod ga pa yod red = Poo kabah yoreh:
a story in Tibetan and English / written and illustrated by Gina Halpern.
p. cm.
Summary: Pema and Tashi, two Tibetan children, go on a spiritual journey to find their home-
land.
Each sentence is written first in the Tibetan alphabet, then phonetically as the Tibetan is
pronounced, then in English.
{1. Tibet–Fiction. 2. Tibetan language materials–Bilingual.}
I. Title. II. Title: Bod ga pa yod red. III. Title: Poo kabah yoreh.
PZ90. T58H3 1991
{E}–dc20   91-9440
                                  CIP
                                  AC

Where Is Tibet?

Tibet is a country located high in the Himalayan mountains. India, China, and Nepal are her neighbors. In the 1950s Tibet was invaded by China. Many Tibetans, including the Dalai Lama, the leader of the Tibetan people, fled to India and Nepal. Today there are Tibetan children growing up in exile wondering where their homeland is. This book celebrates their spirit with hope for peace and restoration in their lifetime. Until that day let us keep the joy and freedom of Tibet alive in our hearts and minds.

Each sentence of this book is written first in the Tibetan alphabet, then as the Tibetan is pronounced, and then in English.
Tibetan translations are by Ngawang Jorden.

ཕྲུ་གུ་འདི་ཚོ་སུ་རེད།

Pugu ditso su reh.

Who are these children?

འདི་པདྨ་རེད།

Di Pema reh.

This is Pema.

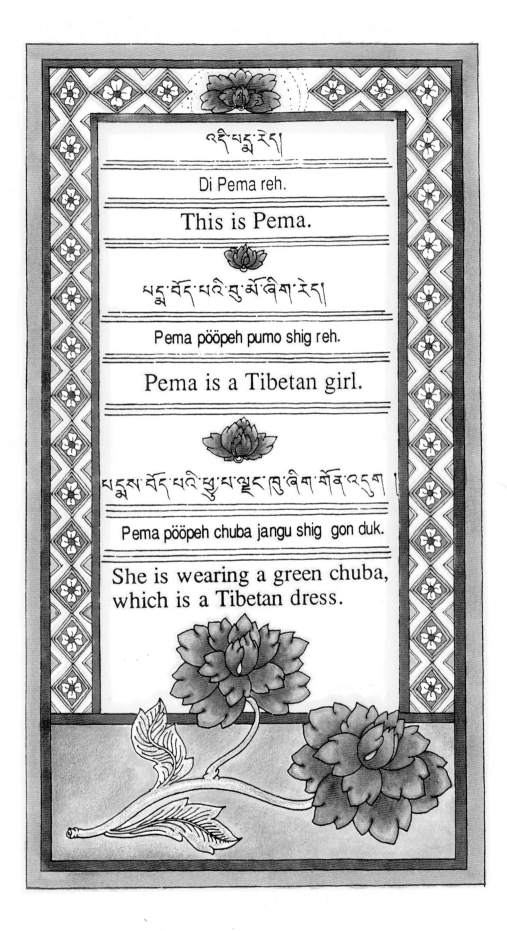

པདྨ་བོད་པའི་བུ་མོ་ཞིག་རེད།

Pema pööpeh pumo shig reh.

Pema is a Tibetan girl.

པདྨས་བོད་པའི་ཕྱུ་པ་ལྗང་ཁུ་ཞིག་གོན་འདུག

Pema pööpeh chuba jangu shig gon duk.

She is wearing a green chuba, which is a Tibetan dress.

འདི་བཀྲ་ཤིས་རེད།

Di Tashi reh.

This is Tashi.

བཀྲ་ཤིས་བོད་པའི་བུ་ཞིག་རེད།

Tashi pööpay pu shig reh.

Tashi is a Tibetan boy.

བཀྲ་ཤིས་ལ་ཞྭ་མོ་སེར་པོ་གཅིག་འདུག

Tashi la shamo serpo chik duk.

Tashi has a yellow hat.

བཀྲ་ཤིས་དང་པདྨ་ཕ་མ་མཉམ་དུ

Tashi dang Pema phama nyamdu

Tashi and Pema live in India

རྒྱ་གར་ལ་སྡོད་ཀྱི་ཡོད་རེད།

gyagar la deh yoreh

with their mother and father,

ཡིན་ན་ཡང་ཁོ་ཚོའི་ཕ་ཡུལ་བོད

yinneh khotshoi phayul Pöö

but their homeland, Tibet,

ཞེ་དྲག་ཐག་རིང་པོ་རེད།

shedrak thak ringpo reh.

is far, far away.

ཉི་མ་གཅིག་ཁོ་ཚོའི་ཕ་མ་ལ་དྲིས་པ་རེད

Nyi ma chik khotshoi phama la dripa reh

One day they ask their parents,

བོད་ག་པ་ཡོད་རེད།

Pöö kabah yoreh?

"Where is Tibet?"

བོད་ག་རེ་བྱས་ནས་དམིགས་བསལ་གྱི་ས་ཆ་རེད།

Pöö gare che nas miksal gyi sacha reh
"Why is Tibet a special place?"

པ་ལ་གས་ཀྱིས་ཕུ་གུ་ཚོ་འདིར་ཤོག་གསུངས།

Pa lak kyi pugu tsho deh shok sung

"Come here, children," says their father,

པང་པའི་སྒང་ལ་ལེན་ནས་

pang pai gang la len neh.

taking them on his lap.

ངས་ཁེད་རང་ཚོར་བོད་ཀྱི་སྐོར་བཤད་གོ་གསུངས།

Ngas khe rang tshor Pöö kyi kor sheh go sung.

"Let me tell you about Tibet."

པ་ལགས་ཀྱིས་བོད་དུ་སྤྲུལ་པའི་འགྲོ་བ་རྣམས་ཡོད་པ་རེད་གསུངས།

Pa lak kyi Pöö du gyu mei do wa nam dod pa reh sung

"Magical beings live in Tibet," says Father,

སྒྲུང་ཞིག་བཤད་གནང་བ་རེད།

dung shik shad nang wa reh.

and he begins to tell a story.

པདྨ་དང་བཀྲ་ཤིས་གཉིས་མིག་བཙུམས་ནས་

Pema dang Tashi nyi mik tsum neh

Pema and Tashi close their eyes

པ་ལགས་ཀྱིས་སུའི་སྐོར་གསུང་གི་ཡོད་པ་བསམ་བློ་བཏང་བ་རེད།

pa lak kyi sui kor sung gi yodpa sam lo dang ba reh.

and imagine who he is talking about.

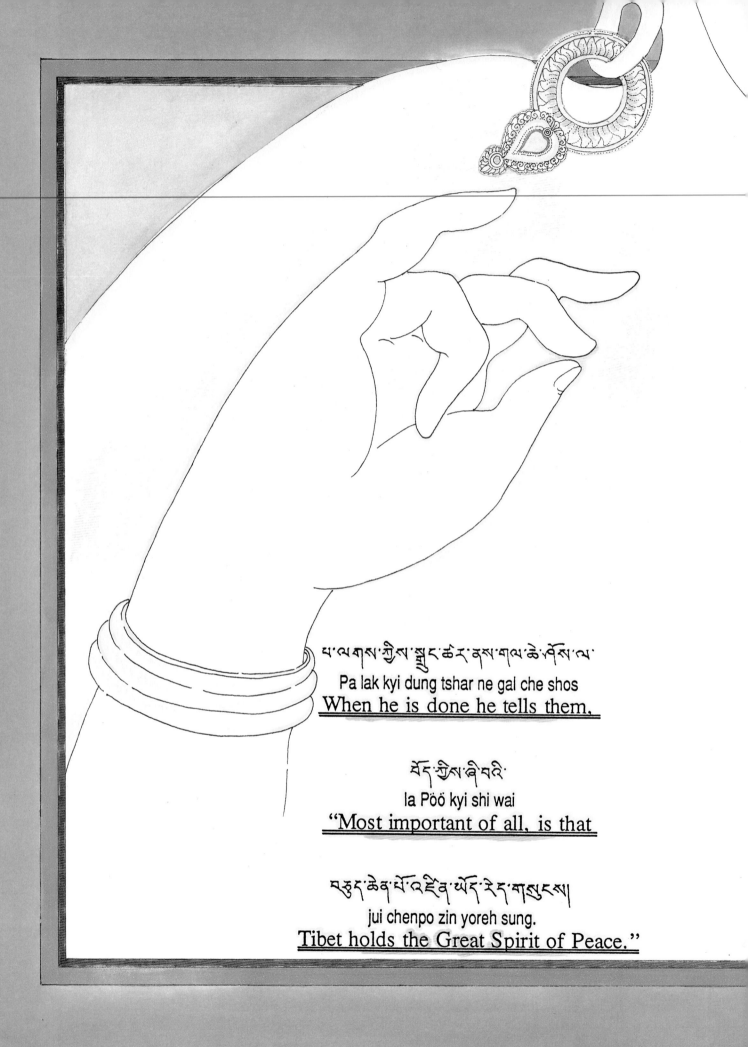

པ་ལ་གས་ཀྱིས་སྦྱུང་ཚར་ནས་གལ་ཆེ་ཤོས་ལ་

Pa lak kyi dung tshar ne gal che shos

<u>When he is done he tells them,</u>

བོད་ཀྱིས་ཞི་བའི་

la Pöö kyi shi wai

<u>"Most important of all, is that</u>

བཅུད་ཆེན་པོ་འཛིན་ཡོད་རེད་གསུངས།

jui chenpo zin yoreh sung.

<u>Tibet holds the Great Spirit of Peace."</u>

བོད་ཞེ་དྲག་ཡག་པོ་ཡོད་ས་རེད། ང་ཚོ་བཙལ་གྱི་ཡིན།

Pöö shey dak yak po yuh sa reh. Nga tshuh tsal gyi yin.

Tibet sounds wonderful. We want to find it.

ཨ་མ་ལགས་ཀྱིས་ཕྱིན་བལ་ལྟོས་གསུངས།

Ama-la kyi chin je tuh sung.

"Go and look," says Mother.

བོད་ཨེ་རྙེད་འཚོལ་ཞིག །

Pöö enye tshol shig.

"See if you can find Tibet."

པ་ཀྲ་ཤིས་དང་པདྨ་གཉིས་བོད་བཙལ་དུ་ཕྱིན་པ་རེད།

Tashi dang Pema nyi Pöö tsal du chinpa reh.

Tashi and Pema set out at once
to see if they can find Tibet.

ཡིན་ནའང་བོ་ཚོས་ག་པ་བཙལ་དགོས་རེད།

Yinneh khotsho gapa tsal goh reh?

But where should they look?

མི་འདུག གཡག་གི་འོག་ལ་ཞི་མི་ཅིག་འདུག

Minduk yak ki ok la shimi chig duk.

No, the cat is under the yak.

བཀྲ་ཤིས་ཀྱིས་ བོད་དཀར་ཡོལ་གྱི་ནང་ལ་འདུག་གམ་ ཞེས་དྲིས་པ་རེད།

Tashi gyi Pöö kayöö gi nang la duk geh sheh dri pa reh?

"Is Tibet in the cup?" asks Tashi.

མི་འདུག། དཀར་ཡོལ་གྱི་ནང་ལ་ཆུ་འདུག།

Minduk kayöö gi nang la chu duk.

No, water is in the cup.

Nya cig chilok la chong ne labpa

A fish jumps out and says,

Pöö day minduk.

"Tibet is not here."

ཞོ་ད་ཊ་དཀར་པོའི་སྐྱ་ར་ལ་འདུག་གས།

Pöö da kar puh gang la duk geh?

Is Tibet on the white horse?

བོད་ཡུང་སྡོང་གི་འོག་ལ་འདུག་གམ།

Pöö shingdong gi ok la duk geh ?

Is Tibet under the tree?

ཤིང་སྡོང་གི་འོག་ལ་སུ་འདུག །

Shingdon gi okla su duk

Who is under the tree?

ཁོང་གི་ཕྱག་ལ་ག་རེ་འདུག

Kong gi chak la kareh duk?

What is in his hand?

In his hand are the moon and stars.

ཕྱུ་གུ་དེ་ཚོ་ནམ་མཁའ་ལ་ཡར་འཕུར་ནས།

Pugu dentsho namka la yar phur neh.

So, up into the sky the children fly.

ཟླ་བ་ལ་དྲིས་པ།

<u>dawa la tree pa</u>

<u>to ask the moon,</u>

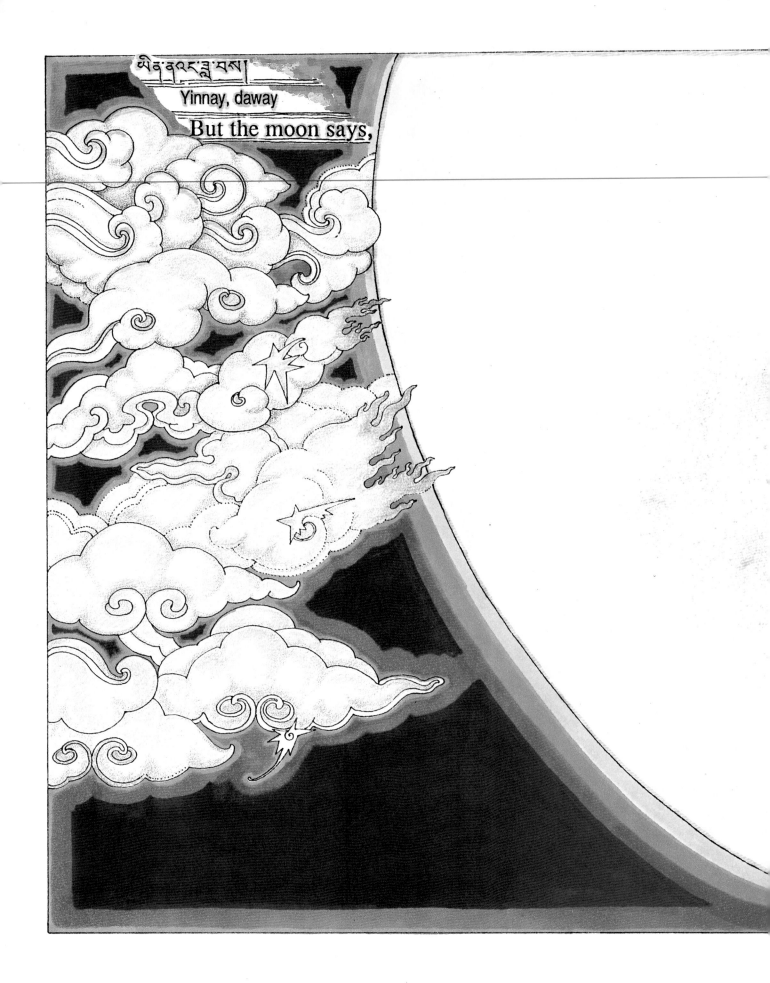

ཨིན་ནའང་ཟླ་བས།

Yinnay, daway

But the moon says,

མི་དེས་ཁྱེད་རང་གིས་སེམས་ལ་ལྟོས་དང་གསུངས་པ་རེད།

Mi deh khyrang gi sem la too dang sung pa reh.

"Look into your mind," the man says.

ཕོད་འདི་ར་འདུག་ག

Pöö day duk.

Here is Tibet.

ཁྱེད་རང་ཚོའི་སེམས་ཀྱི་ནང་ལ་མེ་ཏོག་ནང་བཞིན་སྐྱེ་ཡི་ཡོད་པ་རེད།

Kyrang tshoi sem kyi nang la metog nangshin gyeh gi yoreh.

Growing in your mind like a flower,

དཔེར་ན་མེ་ཏོག་པདྨའི་ནང་ན་རིན་པོ་ཆེ་བཞིན་ནོ།

Perna metog pemai nang na rinpoche shinno.

like a jewel in the Lotus.

བོད་འདིར་འདུག།
Pöö day duk.
Here is Tibet.
སྙིང་ལ་འདུག།
Nying la duk
In your heart,
ཉི་མ་ནང་བཞིན་འདུག།
Nyima nang shin yoreh.
like the sun.

ཁྱེད་ཀྱི་སེམས་ལ་སྙིང་རྗེ་གང་བར་ཤོག

Khyeh gyi sem la nying jeh kang war shok.

May your heart be full of compassion.

ཁྱེད་ཀྱི་སེམས་ལ་ཡེ་ཤེས་སྐྱེ་བར་ཤོག

Khyeh gyi sem la yeshe kye war shok.

May your mind grow in wisdom.

English Alphabet

Aa Bb Cc

Dd Ee Ff

Gg Hh Ii Jj

Kk Ll Mm

Nn Oo Pp

Qq Rr Ss

Tt Uu Vv

Ww Xx Yy

Zz

Tibetan Alphabet

kā	kā	ka	nga
chā	chā	cha	nya
tā	tā	ta	na
pā	pā	pa	ma
dza	tzā	tsa	wa
shar	sa	a	ya
ra	la	shā	sā

i	u	hā	ā	e	o

This book is
dedicated to the
children
and
to all those
who work for peace
on earth,
with special appreciation
for the inspiration of
His Holiness
the Dalai Lama of Tibet

*Created
with much love
and with many thanks for support and encouragement to:
Tara Doyle for bringing me to Bodhgaya, Katie Mitchell, David Jackson,
Arianne Dworsky-Dar, Lindy Wielblad,
Jesse McCormick, and
all my Dear Ones.*